Book of Shadows
Property Of :

_____

Begun on this day:

_____

Book of Shadows Protection

Ye old book of shadows belongs to me, so thy hands thou must keep free. Please leave this book as it was found, or bad luck on the will abound. This is not my wish but thee be warned, your fate you make if this book is scorned. So respect this book if you please, or thou shall test the rule of three.

Book of Shadows Blessing

Hearken as the Witch's word
Calls the lady and the lord
Moon above and earth below
In this right and ready hour
May no unprepared eye to see
The secrets which trusted be
To I who walk the hidden road
To find the hearthstone 's calm abode
Hear me and lend they protection
May these truths of earth and sky
Shaded be from prying eyes
But to the witch whose map this be
May the way be plain to see
And through all the coming ages
May we find home in these pages
So mote it be

Full Lunar cycle

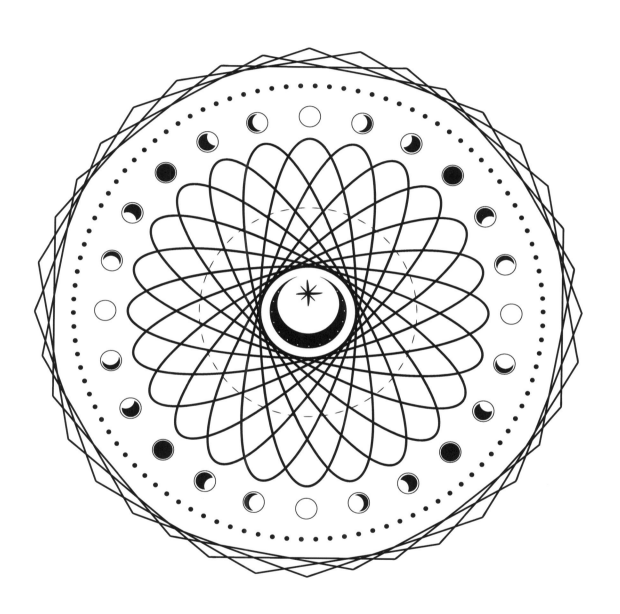

Wheel of the Year

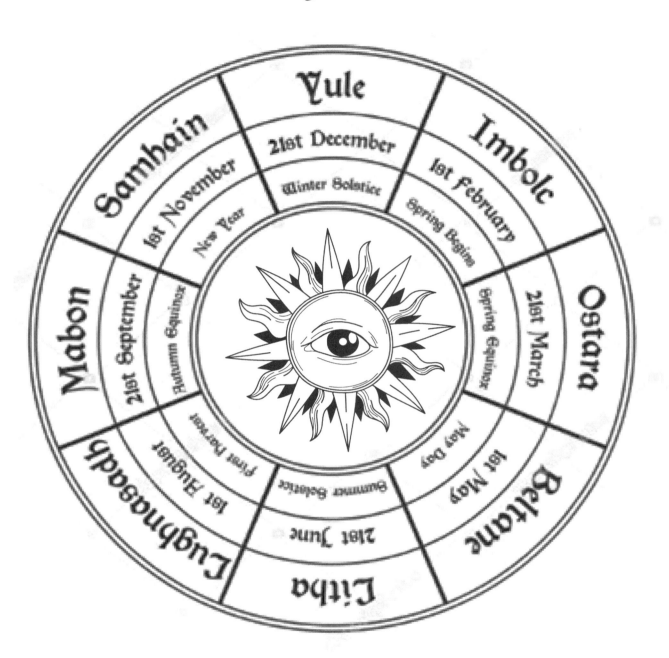

HOW TO CELEBRATE THE WHEEL OF THE YEAR

Learning to use the Wheel of the Year can feel overwhelming, but the way that you work with it can be as simple or complex as you want it to be. There are many different ways to celebrate each occasion on the Wheel of the Year. Check out the list below for a list of ways you can enjoy the Wheel of the Year.

- Spend time outside in nature.

- Attend a local celebration or create your own for some or all festivals.

- Conduct a ritual for each Sabbat. You can find several ritual examples for each Sabbat by searching the Sabbat on our blog.

- Add decor and scents to your house based on the Wheel of the Year.

- Cleanse and update your sacred space for each Sabbat.

- Cook specific foods for each of the Sabbats.

Five Elements

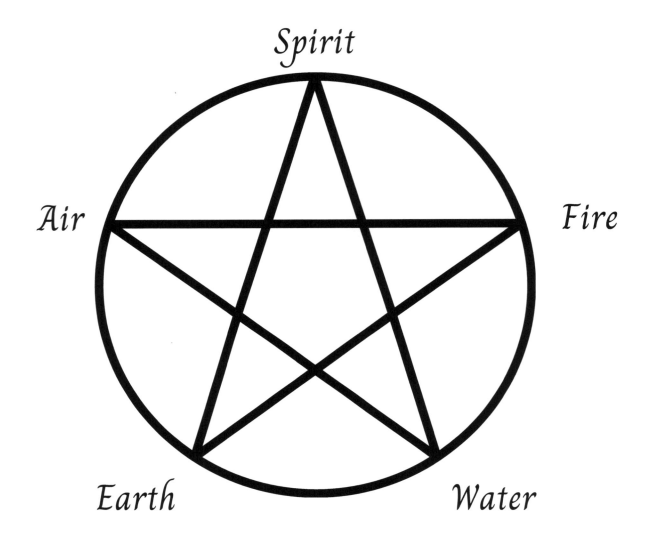

Five Elements

Earth - Green

Matter, foundation, manifestation, money, incorporating, employment, touch, empathy, understanding, fertility, security, safety, home, prosperity, and business. Represents stability and physical endurance.

Air - Yellow

Thought, creativity, knowledge, mental activity, study, speech, intellect, ideas, communication, hearing, travel, messages, eloquence, freedom, discovery, revealing hidden things, and secrets. Represents intelligence and the arts.

Fire - Red

Energy, spirituality, passions, light, vitality, health, goals, desires, destiny, sexuality, purification, and sight. Represents courage and daring.

Water - Blue

Feelings, happiness, pleasure, love, children, friendship, marriage, family, ancestors, veils, home, taste, dreams, sleep, divination, purification, cleansings, healing, psychic and intuition, and the sub-conscious. Represents emotions and intuition.

Spirit - White

Spiritual energy, magick, empowerment, community, purpose, divine connections, interconnections, power. Represents the All, Deity, and the blending of the Elements.

Spell and Ritual Worksheet

Goal/Purpose

Date:_____

Day of Week:_____

Moon Phase:_____

Purpose:_____

Materials and ingredients

_____
_____
_____
_____
_____
_____
_____
_____
_____

Invocations:

_____
_____
_____
_____
_____
_____
_____
_____
_____

After this Ritual I feel:

Place:

Instructions:

Results:

Modifications

Spell and Ritual Worksheet

Goal/Purpose

Date:_____

Day of Week:_____

Moon Phase:_____

Purpose:_____

Invocations:

Materials and ingredients

_____
_____
_____
_____
_____
_____
_____
_____
_____

_____
_____
_____
_____
_____
_____
_____
_____

After this Ritual I feel:

Place:

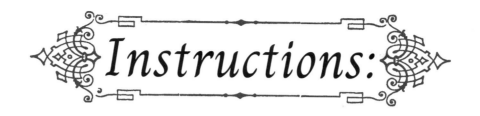

Instructions:

Results:

Modifications

Spell and Ritual Worksheet

Goal/Purpose

Date:_____

Day of Week:_____

Moon Phase:_____

Purpose:_____

Materials and ingredients

_____
_____
_____
_____
_____
_____
_____
_____
_____

Invocations:

_____
_____
_____
_____
_____
_____
_____
_____

After this Ritual I feel:

Place:

Instructions:

Results:

Modifications

Spell and Ritual Worksheet

Goal/Purpose

Date:_____

Day of Week:_____

Moon Phase:_____

Purpose:_____

Materials and ingredients

_____
_____
_____
_____
_____
_____
_____
_____
_____

Invocations:

_____
_____
_____
_____
_____
_____
_____
_____
_____
_____

After this Ritual I feel:

Place:

Instructions:

Results:

Modifications

Spell and Ritual Worksheet

Goal/Purpose

Date:_____

Day of Week:_____

Moon Phase:_____

Purpose:_____

Materials and ingredients

_____

_____

_____

_____

_____

_____

_____

_____

_____

Invocations:

_____

_____

_____

_____

_____

_____

_____

_____

After this Ritual I feel:

Place:

Instructions:

Results:

Modifications

Spell and Ritual Worksheet

Goal/Purpose

Date:_____

Day of Week:_____

Moon Phase:_____

Purpose:_____

Invocations:

Materials and ingredients

_____
_____
_____
_____
_____
_____
_____
_____
_____

_____
_____
_____
_____
_____
_____
_____
_____

After this Ritual I feel:

Place:

Instructions:

Results:

Modifications

Spell and Ritual Worksheet

Goal/Purpose

Date:_____

Day of Week:_____

Moon Phase:_____

Purpose:_____

Invocations:

Materials and ingredients

_____

_____

_____

_____

_____

_____

_____

_____

_____

_____

_____

_____

_____

_____

_____

_____

After this Ritual I feel:

Place:

Instructions:

Results:

Modifications

Spell and Ritual Worksheet

Goal/Purpose

Date:_____

Day of Week:_____

Moon Phase:_____

Purpose:_____

Materials and ingredients

_____
_____
_____
_____
_____
_____
_____
_____
_____

Invocations:

_____
_____
_____
_____
_____
_____
_____
_____
_____

After this Ritual I feel:

Place:

Instructions:

Results:

Modifications

Spell and Ritual Worksheet

Goal/Purpose

Date:_____

Day of Week:_____

Moon Phase:_____

Purpose:_____

Materials and ingredients

_____
_____
_____
_____
_____
_____
_____
_____
_____

Invocations:

_____
_____
_____
_____
_____
_____
_____
_____
_____

After this Ritual I feel:

Place:

Instructions:

Results:

Modifications

Spell and Ritual Worksheet

Goal/Purpose

Date:_____

Day of Week:_____

Moon Phase:_____

Purpose:_____

Materials and ingredients

_____
_____
_____
_____
_____
_____
_____
_____
_____

Invocations:

_____
_____
_____
_____
_____
_____
_____
_____

After this Ritual I feel:

Place:

Instructions:

Results:

Modifications

Spell and Ritual Worksheet

Goal/Purpose

Date:_____

Day of Week:_____

Moon Phase:_____

Purpose:_____

Materials and ingredients

_____
_____
_____
_____
_____
_____
_____
_____
_____
_____

Invocations:

_____
_____
_____
_____
_____
_____
_____
_____
_____

After this Ritual I feel:

Place:

Instructions:

Results:

Modifications

Spell and Ritual Worksheet

Goal/Purpose

Date:_____

Day of Week:_____

Moon Phase:_____

Purpose:_____

Materials and ingredients

_____
_____
_____
_____
_____
_____
_____
_____
_____

Invocations:

_____
_____
_____
_____
_____
_____
_____
_____

After this Ritual I feel:

Place:

Instructions:

Results:

Modifications

Spell and Ritual Worksheet

Goal/Purpose

Date:_____

Day of Week:_____

Moon Phase:_____

Materials and ingredients

_____

_____

_____

_____

_____

_____

_____

_____

_____

_____

Purpose:_____

Invocations:

_____

_____

_____

_____

_____

_____

_____

_____

_____

After this Ritual I feel:

Place:

Instructions:

Results:

Modifications

Spell and Ritual Worksheet

Goal/Purpose

Date:_____

Day of Week:_____

Moon Phase:_____

Purpose:_____

Materials and ingredients

_____
_____
_____
_____
_____
_____
_____
_____
_____

Invocations:

_____
_____
_____
_____
_____
_____
_____
_____

After this Ritual I feel:

Place:

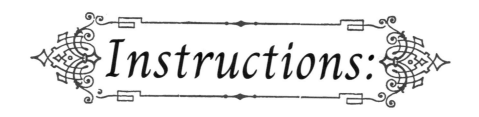

Instructions:

Results:

Modifications

Spell and Ritual Worksheet

Goal/Purpose

Date:_____

Day of Week:_____

Moon Phase:_____

Purpose:_____

Materials and ingredients

_____

_____

_____

_____

_____

_____

_____

_____

_____

Invocations:

_____

_____

_____

_____

_____

_____

_____

_____

After this Ritual I feel:

Place:

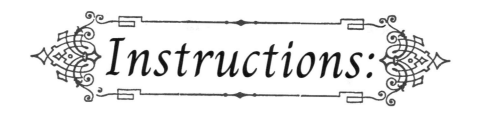

Instructions:

Results:

Modifications

Spell and Ritual Worksheet

Goal/Purpose

Date:_____

Day of Week:_____

Moon Phase:_____

Purpose:_____

Materials and ingredients

_____
_____
_____
_____
_____
_____
_____
_____
_____

Invocations:

_____
_____
_____
_____
_____
_____
_____
_____

After this Ritual I feel:

Place:

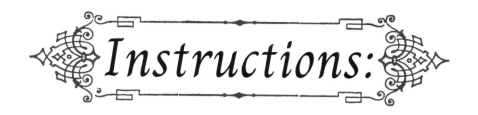

Instructions:

Results:

Modifications

Spell and Ritual Worksheet

Goal/Purpose

Date:_____

Day of Week:_____

Moon Phase:_____

Purpose:_____

Materials and ingredients

_____
_____
_____
_____
_____
_____
_____
_____
_____

Invocations:

_____
_____
_____
_____
_____
_____
_____
_____
_____

After this Ritual I feel:

Place:

Instructions:

Results:

Modifications

Spell and Ritual Worksheet

Goal/Purpose

Date:_____

Day of Week:_____

Moon Phase:_____

Purpose:_____

Materials and ingredients

_____
_____
_____
_____
_____
_____
_____
_____
_____

Invocations:

_____
_____
_____
_____
_____
_____
_____
_____
_____

After this Ritual I feel:

Place:

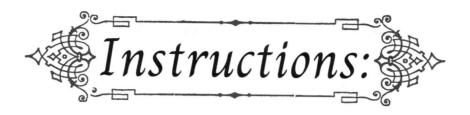

Instructions:

Results:

Modifications

Spell and Ritual Worksheet

Goal/Purpose

Date:_____

Day of Week:_____

Moon Phase:_____

Purpose:_____

Invocations:

_____

_____

_____

_____

_____

_____

_____

_____

_____

Materials and ingredients

_____

_____

_____

_____

_____

_____

_____

_____

_____

_____

After this Ritual I feel:

Place:

Instructions:

Results:

Modifications

Spell and Ritual Worksheet

Goal/Purpose

Date:_____

Day of Week:_____

Moon Phase:_____

Purpose:_____

Materials and ingredients

_____
_____
_____
_____
_____
_____
_____
_____
_____
_____

Invocations:

_____
_____
_____
_____
_____
_____
_____
_____
_____
_____

After this Ritual I feel:

Place:

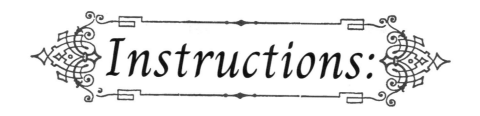

Instructions:

Results:

Modifications

Spell and Ritual Worksheet

Goal/Purpose

Date:_____

Day of Week:_____

Moon Phase:_____

Purpose:_____

Materials and ingredients

_____
_____
_____
_____
_____
_____
_____
_____
_____
_____

Invocations:

_____
_____
_____
_____
_____
_____
_____
_____
_____

After this Ritual I feel:

Place:

Instructions:

Results:

Modifications

Spell and Ritual Worksheet

Goal/Purpose

Date:_____

Day of Week:_____

Moon Phase:_____

Purpose:_____

Materials and ingredients

_____
_____
_____
_____
_____
_____
_____
_____
_____

Invocations:

_____
_____
_____
_____
_____
_____
_____
_____

After this Ritual I feel:

Place:

 Instructions:

Results:

Modifications

Spell and Ritual Worksheet

Goal/Purpose

Date:_____

Day of Week:_____

Moon Phase:_____

Purpose:_____

Materials and ingredients

_____
_____
_____
_____
_____
_____
_____
_____
_____
_____

Invocations:

_____
_____
_____
_____
_____
_____
_____
_____

After this Ritual I feel:

Place:

Instructions:

Results:

Modifications

Spell and Ritual Worksheet

Goal/Purpose

Date:_____

Day of Week:_____

Moon Phase:_____

Materials and ingredients

Purpose:_____

Invocations:

_____

_____

_____

_____

_____

_____

_____

_____

_____

_____

_____

_____

_____

_____

_____

After this Ritual I feel:

Place:

Instructions:

Results:

Modifications

Spell and Ritual Worksheet

Goal/Purpose

Date:_____

Day of Week:_____

Moon Phase:_____

Purpose:_____

Materials and ingredients

Invocations:

_____
_____
_____
_____
_____
_____
_____
_____
_____

_____
_____
_____
_____
_____
_____
_____
_____
_____

After this Ritual I feel:

Place:

Instructions:

Results:

Modifications

Spell and Ritual Worksheet

Goal/Purpose

Date:_____

Day of Week:_____

Moon Phase:_____

Purpose:_____

Materials and ingredients

_____

_____

_____

_____

_____

_____

_____

_____

_____

_____

Invocations:

_____

_____

_____

_____

_____

_____

_____

_____

_____

After this Ritual I feel:

Place:

Instructions:

Results:

Modifications

Spell and Ritual Worksheet

Goal/Purpose

Date:_____

Day of Week:_____

Moon Phase:_____

Purpose:_____

Invocations:

_____

_____

_____

_____

_____

_____

_____

_____

Materials and ingredients

_____

_____

_____

_____

_____

_____

_____

_____

_____

_____

After this Ritual I feel:

Place:

Instructions:

Results:

Modifications

Spell and Ritual Worksheet

Goal/Purpose

Date:_____

Day of Week:_____

Moon Phase:_____

Purpose:_____

Materials and ingredients

_____

_____

_____

_____

_____

_____

_____

_____

_____

Invocations:

_____

_____

_____

_____

_____

_____

_____

_____

After this Ritual I feel:

Place:

Instructions:

Results:

Modifications

Spell and Ritual Worksheet

Goal/Purpose

Date:_____

Day of Week:_____

Moon Phase:_____

Purpose:_____

Materials and ingredients

_____
_____
_____
_____
_____
_____
_____
_____
_____
_____

Invocations:

_____
_____
_____
_____
_____
_____
_____
_____

After this Ritual I feel:

Place:

Instructions:

Results:

Modifications

Spell and Ritual Worksheet

Goal/Purpose

Date:_____

Day of Week:_____

Moon Phase:_____

Purpose:_____

Materials and ingredients

_____
_____
_____
_____
_____
_____
_____
_____
_____
_____

Invocations:

_____
_____
_____
_____
_____
_____
_____
_____
_____

After this Ritual I feel:

Place:

Instructions:

Results:

Modifications

Spell and Ritual Worksheet

Goal/Purpose

Date:_____

Day of Week:_____

Moon Phase:_____

Purpose:_____

Materials and ingredients

_____
_____
_____
_____
_____
_____
_____
_____
_____

Invocations:

_____
_____
_____
_____
_____
_____
_____
_____

After this Ritual I feel:

Place:

Instructions:

Results:

Modifications

Spell and Ritual Worksheet

Goal/Purpose

Date:_____

Day of Week:_____

Moon Phase:_____

Purpose:_____

Materials and ingredients

_____
_____
_____
_____
_____
_____
_____
_____
_____

Invocations:

_____
_____
_____
_____
_____
_____
_____
_____
_____

After this Ritual I feel:

Place:

Instructions:

Results:

Modifications

Spell and Ritual Worksheet

Goal/Purpose

Date:_____

Day of Week:_____

Moon Phase:_____

Purpose:_____

Invocations:

_____
_____
_____
_____
_____
_____
_____
_____
_____

Materials and ingredients

_____
_____
_____
_____
_____
_____
_____
_____
_____
_____

After this Ritual I feel:

Place:

Instructions:

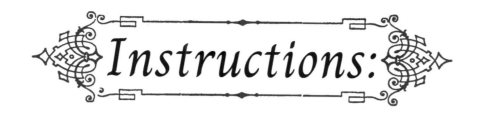

Results:

Modifications

Spell and Ritual Worksheet

Goal/Purpose

Date:_____

Day of Week:_____

Moon Phase:_____

Purpose:_____

Materials and ingredients

_____

_____

_____

_____

_____

_____

_____

_____

Invocations:

_____

_____

_____

_____

_____

_____

After this Ritual I feel:

Place:

Instructions:

Results:

Modifications

Spell and Ritual Worksheet

Goal/Purpose

Date:_____

Day of Week:_____

Moon Phase:_____

Purpose:_____

Materials and ingredients

_____
_____
_____
_____
_____
_____
_____
_____
_____

Invocations:

_____
_____
_____
_____
_____
_____
_____
_____
_____

After this Ritual I feel:

Place:

Instructions:

Results:

Modifications

Spell and Ritual Worksheet

Goal/Purpose

Date:_____

Day of Week:_____

Moon Phase:_____

Purpose:_____

Invocations:

Materials and ingredients

_____

_____

_____

_____

_____

_____

_____

_____

_____

_____

_____

_____

_____

_____

_____

_____

_____

After this Ritual I feel:

Place:

Instructions:

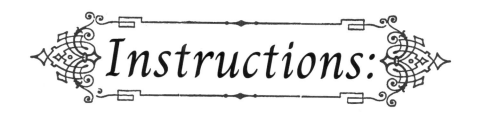

Results:

Modifications

Spell and Ritual Worksheet

Goal/Purpose

Date:_____

Day of Week:_____

Moon Phase:_____

Materials and ingredients

Purpose:_____

Invocations:

_____

_____

_____

_____

_____

_____

_____

_____

_____

_____

_____

_____

_____

_____

_____

After this Ritual I feel:

Place:

Instructions:

Results:

Modifications

Spell and Ritual Worksheet

Goal/Purpose

Date:_____

Day of Week:_____

Moon Phase:_____

Purpose:_____

Materials and ingredients

_____
_____
_____
_____
_____
_____
_____
_____
_____

Invocations:

_____
_____
_____
_____
_____
_____
_____
_____

After this Ritual I feel:

Place:

Instructions:

Results:

Modifications

Spell and Ritual Worksheet

Goal/Purpose

Date:_____

Day of Week:_____

Moon Phase:_____

Purpose:_____

Materials and ingredients

_____
_____
_____
_____
_____
_____
_____
_____
_____

Invocations:

_____
_____
_____
_____
_____
_____
_____
_____
_____

After this Ritual I feel:

Place:

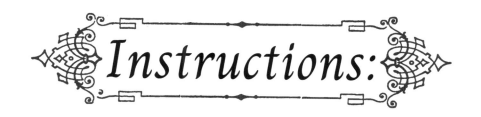 Instructions:

Results:

Modifications

Spell and Ritual Worksheet

Goal/Purpose

Date:_____

Day of Week:_____

Moon Phase:_____

Purpose:_____

Materials and ingredients

_____
_____
_____
_____
_____
_____
_____
_____
_____

Invocations:

_____
_____
_____
_____
_____
_____
_____
_____

After this Ritual I feel:

Place:

Instructions:

Results:

Modifications

Spell and Ritual Worksheet

Goal/Purpose

Date:_____

Day of Week:_____

Moon Phase:_____

Purpose:_____

Materials and ingredients

_____
_____
_____
_____
_____
_____
_____
_____

Invocations:

_____
_____
_____
_____
_____
_____
_____
_____

After this Ritual I feel:

Place:

Instructions:

Results:

Modifications

Spell and Ritual Worksheet

Goal/Purpose

Date:_____

Day of Week:_____

Moon Phase:_____

Purpose:_____

Invocations:

Materials and ingredients

_____
_____
_____
_____
_____
_____
_____
_____
_____

_____
_____
_____
_____
_____
_____
_____
_____
_____

After this Ritual I feel:

Place:

Instructions:

Results:

Modifications

Spell and Ritual Worksheet

Goal/Purpose

Date:_____

Day of Week:_____

Moon Phase:_____

Purpose:_____

Materials and ingredients

_____
_____
_____
_____
_____
_____
_____
_____
_____

Invocations:

_____
_____
_____
_____
_____
_____
_____
_____

After this Ritual I feel:

Place:

Instructions:

Results:

Modifications

Spell and Ritual Worksheet

Goal/Purpose

Date:_____

Day of Week:_____

Moon Phase:_____

Purpose:_____

Materials and ingredients

_____
_____
_____
_____
_____
_____
_____
_____
_____

Invocations:

_____
_____
_____
_____
_____
_____
_____
_____

After this Ritual I feel:

Place:

Instructions:

Results:

Modifications

Spell and Ritual Worksheet

Goal/Purpose

Date:_____

Day of Week:_____

Moon Phase:_____

Materials and ingredients

Purpose:_____

_____

_____

Invocations:

_____

_____

_____

_____

_____

_____

_____

_____

_____

_____

_____

_____

_____

_____

After this Ritual I feel:

Place:

Instructions:

Results:

Modifications

Spell and Ritual Worksheet

Goal/Purpose

Date:_____

Day of Week:_____

Moon Phase:_____

Purpose:_____

Materials and ingredients

_____
_____
_____
_____
_____
_____
_____
_____
_____
_____

Invocations:

_____
_____
_____
_____
_____
_____
_____
_____
_____
_____

After this Ritual I feel:

Place:

Instructions:

Results:

Modifications

Spell and Ritual Worksheet

Goal/Purpose

Date:_____

Day of Week:_____

Moon Phase:_____

Purpose:_____

Materials and ingredients

_____
_____
_____
_____
_____
_____
_____
_____
_____
_____

Invocations:

_____
_____
_____
_____
_____
_____
_____
_____
_____

After this Ritual I feel:

Place:

Instructions:

Results:

Modifications

Spell and Ritual Worksheet

Goal/Purpose

Date:_____

Day of Week:_____

Moon Phase:_____

Purpose:_____

Materials and ingredients

_____
_____
_____
_____
_____
_____
_____
_____
_____
_____

Invocations:

_____
_____
_____
_____
_____
_____
_____
_____
_____
_____

After this Ritual I feel:

Place:

Instructions:

Results:

Modifications

Spell and Ritual Worksheet

Goal/Purpose

Date:_____

Day of Week:_____

Moon Phase:_____

Purpose:_____

Materials and ingredients

_____
_____
_____
_____
_____
_____
_____
_____
_____

Invocations:

_____
_____
_____
_____
_____
_____
_____
_____

After this Ritual I feel:

Place:

Instructions:

Results:

Modifications

Spell and Ritual Worksheet

Goal/Purpose

Date:_____

Day of Week:_____

Moon Phase:_____

Purpose:_____

Invocations:

Materials and ingredients

_____
_____
_____
_____
_____
_____
_____
_____
_____
_____

_____
_____
_____
_____
_____
_____
_____
_____
_____
_____

After this Ritual I feel:

Place:

Instructions:

Results:

Modifications

Spell and Ritual Worksheet

Goal/Purpose

Date:_____

Day of Week:_____

Moon Phase:_____

Purpose:_____

Materials and ingredients

Invocations:

_____

_____

_____

_____

_____

_____

_____

_____

_____

_____

_____

_____

_____

_____

_____

_____

_____

_____

After this Ritual I feel:

Place:

Instructions:

Results:

Modifications

Spell and Ritual Worksheet

Goal/Purpose

Date:_____

Day of Week:_____

Moon Phase:_____

Purpose:_____

Materials and ingredients

_____
_____
_____
_____
_____
_____
_____
_____
_____

Invocations:

_____
_____
_____
_____
_____
_____
_____
_____

After this Ritual I feel:

Place:

Instructions:

Results:

Modifications

Spell and Ritual Worksheet

Goal/Purpose

Date:_____

Day of Week:_____

Moon Phase:_____

Purpose:_____

Materials and ingredients

_____

_____

_____

_____

_____

_____

_____

_____

_____

_____

Invocations:

_____

_____

_____

_____

_____

_____

_____

_____

After this Ritual I feel:

Place:

Instructions:

Results:

Modifications

Spell and Ritual Worksheet

Goal/Purpose

Date:_____

Day of Week:_____

Moon Phase:_____

Purpose:_____

Materials and ingredients

_____
_____
_____
_____
_____
_____
_____
_____
_____

Invocations:

_____
_____
_____
_____
_____
_____
_____
_____
_____

After this Ritual I feel:

Place:

Instructions:

Results:

Modifications

Printed in Great Britain
by Amazon

37227218R00070